FRIDGE
OVER
TROUBLED
WATER

THE AUTHOR Judy Rose was born in London in 1956. She started writing poems in 1993 and for the past year has been reading them every fortnight on BBC Radio Gloucestershire. She lives in the Cotswolds where she and her husband run a travel publishing business and farm llamas. They have two sons.

To my parents,
Pamela and David Kroll,
with love

FRIDGE OVER TROUBLED WATER

A Collection of Poems

JUDY ROSE

THE WINDRUSH PRESS · GLOUCESTERSHIRE

First published in Great Britain in 1995 by
The Windrush Press Limited
Little Window, High Street
Moreton-in-Marsh
Gloucestershire GL56 0LL

Telephone 01608 652012
Fax 01608 652125

British Library Cataloguing in Publication Data
A catalogue record for this book is available from
the British Library

ISBN 0 900075 39 2

Typeset by Archetype, Stow-on-the-Wold
Printed and bound in Great Britain by Bell & Bain Ltd, Glasgow

Contents

Tales from the Domestic Front

Trials and Tribulations

The Festive Season

The Body . . .
Not so Beautiful

Beauty and the Beach

It's two weeks to my holiday, the annual great escape,
And I have to say, objectively, the body's in poor shape.
The time has come to cast aside the thermal underwear
But that which lurks beneath it, really fills me with despair.
The only thing to help me now is pretty drastic action . . .
Like a spot of plastic surgery . . . or maybe liposuction?
I've got no time to mess around, I need to act and quick;
Now a thigh and buttock transplant . . . that would really do the
   trick.
The magazines are full of ways to shape up for the beach
But 'You've got to start well in advance' is the message that they
   preach.
Well, time is getting very short, these warnings were ignored,
The 'beauty countdown to the sun' I fear's gone by the board.
I'd love to get all lithe and fit, promote that healthy tan,
But a miracle is what I need . . . not a six-week toning plan.
Crash diets are an option, as I have a stone to lose,
But you need a lot of self-control, so it's not one I would choose.
And then there's always working-out, but on the whole I've found
That I don't get rid of all that flab . . . but just shift it around.
I could always do some groundwork for that even golden tan
Exfoliating, earnestly, as often as I can.
Or what about a sun bed? Surely that is worth a try?
It makes your skin feel sun-kissed, not to mention crisp and dry.
And as for all that cellulite, I must get shot of that . . .
To recap on my problems . . . I AM LUMPY, PALE AND FAT!
I tried on my bikini – a foolish move I know –
A femme fatale – without the 'ale' – no wonder morale's low.
I knew there was no hope for me, I'd left it all too late;
To be Ms Beached Whale '95 will have to be my fate.

3

Tipping the Scales

This morning when I weighed myself
I got an awful fright . . .
For the weight that came up on the dial
Was certainly not right.
I've really had it with these scales,
They're utterly misleading,
I slid them over to the bath
To get a second reading.
Again the weight that registered
Was ridiculously high,
I moved them back towards the loo
To have another try.
The pointer stubbornly remained
Just under ten stone three . . .
I raised one foot and then breathed in
But all quite fruitlessly.
My last hope was the carpet
So I moved to softer ground,
Just to suffer more frustration –
I had gained another pound.
I'll really have to face the fact
These scales have had their day;
They simply can't deliver me
An honest, spot-on weigh.
A brand-new, high-tech digital
Would really be the bizz;
I need top-notch equipment now
That 'tells it like it is'.
And passing by the mirror
I catch sight of my reflection,

It's not a picture that inspires
A more in-depth inspection,
But I am not perturbed at all
At the vision that appears . . .
That mirror distorts everything . . .
It's been like that for years.

Survival of the Fattest

I squeezed my plumpish form
Into the lycra leotard,
Although a stretchy fabric
I still found this somewhat hard.
And then the matching leggings
Though in retrospect I think
In many ways it wasn't wise,
To opt for 'dayglo' pink.
Then towelling socks and trainers
Yes, all kitted out in style . . .
I gazed at my reflection
In horror
For some while.

Yet undeterred I joined the class
Of super-fit nymphets
Not walking out at once is still
One of my great regrets.
The thirtysomething model
Who has had no exercise . . .
That striking lack of muscle tone
That flab one can't disguise.
Aerobotically speaking
I could simply not ignore
All these bodies were the 'after'
Whereas mine was
The 'before'.

Oh how I blushed and how I cringed
As I failed to keep the pace
My unco-ordinated jerks
A source of deep disgrace.
We pulled and pushed, we stretched and squeezed,
We worked up quite a sweat,
And the moment when my lycra gave
Is one I won't forget.
And yet I saw this torture through
Until its bitter end,
Just praying that eventually
My broken bits
Would mend.

How I made it to the changing room
Well, heaven only knows;
In a heap of bright pink lycra
I just sat there . . . comatose.
Next morning I did wonder
Why on earth I had persisted;
I ached in places up till then
I didn't know existed.
This working out just can't be right . . .
There's too much pain and grind . . .
I think I'll let my body go . . .
Just exercise
My mind . . .

Never Say Diet

Breakfast

I've weighed my ounce of cereal, the skimmed milk's measured
  out,
I've performed this ritual many times, so I know what I'm about,
There's tea, no milk, no sugar and half a grapefruit too . . .
Yes, it's day one of my diet . . . I've a sense of *déjà vu*.
By ten o'clock the hunger pangs are getting very strong,
I need a little sustenance to help me get along . . .
The biscuit-tin is beckoning . . . I need a chocolate fix
(There can't be many calories in this tiny little Twix)

Lunch

I've weighed with great precision two thin slices of brown bread
And coated them so sparingly with very low-fat spread,
I've got my ounce of cottage cheese, two slices of lean ham,
(But I'm dreaming of two doorsteps very thickly spread with jam)
As light snacks go, a sandwich is, of course, quite hard to beat,
But I cannot really say that I am feeling that replete.
And then I spot the sweetie jar, just have a little delve
I check my watch and notice it is twenty-five to twelve . . .

Tea

I've walked the dog, I've washed the car, I've made the place look
  neat,
Anything to take my mind off all the food I cannot eat,

I've dusted all my ornaments and read the papers . . . twice.
I'm ready for a cup of tea . . . with something very nice.
(A pack of milk digestives would really fit the bill,
Or three éclairs, or a loaf of bread, or a very large mixed grill)
But it's day one of my diet . . . and I have to see this through;
I have a stick of celery . . . and a bag of crisps or two.

Supper

I've steamed up lots of vegetables to make that slimming soup,
(But my mind is in the freezer with that litre of soft scoop)
The slimming magazines all say 'prepare your meals with care',
So I've laid out my two lettuce leaves with quite a lot of flair.
On these I place an appetising skinless chicken leg
(But what would have much more appeal is sausage, bacon,
    egg . . .)
And now that slimmer's pudding . . . I'll really pig on that . . .
A kiwi and some seedless grapes and yoghurt . . . yes low-fat.
And so I slowly savour this, my last meal of the day
Hallucinating all the while of a Chinese Take-Away.

My dreams that night are yes . . . you guessed . . . of all forbidden
    food,
I wake up feeling hungry and in very sombre mood.
I mount the scales and lo! no change after all that self-control . . .
I console myself with a Kit-Kat, a Bounty and choc-roll.
And then of course I hate myself, all awash with rage and sorrow
So I quickly finish off that loaf . . . and I'll start, for real, tomorrow!

The Pencil Test

To find out if you're firm and pert of breast
Or so the women's magazines all say
You really have to do 'the pencil test'
I'm told this is the only foolproof way.
You'd think, by looking, you could surely tell
And this old pencil lark seemed quite bizarre
But then one day I thought 'oh what the hell'
And recklessly removed my well-wired bra.
To my chagrin, the pencil stayed in place
Instead of dropping down on to the floor
I found this outcome somewhat hard to face;
I then tried with a felt pen to make sure.
I failed again and though I was displeased . . .
I've found a handy place to keep HBs.

Shopping with the Enemy

Communal changing-room. This is a blow.
Morale's not great. I'm feeling fat and old
And really not in mood to boldly go
And share with girls in flab-free-Kate-Moss mould.

With graceful ease they'll slip into size eight.
Each outfit will just suit them to perfection.
For them no thoughts of 'God, I must lose weight'
No breathing in, in front of their reflection.

For them no heaving chests and hot flushed faces
From struggling with those 'very stubborn' zips.
For them no clothes that cling in the wrong places,
Or worse – that get stuck half-way up the hips.

Such changing-room-mates I can do without;
They do so little for one's self-esteem.
And leave the likes of me in little doubt
As to my being fashion's sweet young dream.

If share I must, bring those of 'fuller figure',
Whose 'best by' date is now past history,
Who says things like 'Does this come any bigger?'
Has cellulite and wobbly bits like me.

We'll shyly smile in friendly recognition
On seeing bodies not unlike our own,
Acknowledging our tricky common mission;
To clothe her who is 'more than skin and bone'.

11

Nice Clothes . . . Shame about the Body

The sales assistant young and lean, and yes, a perfect eight,
Is trying hard to kit me out for 'that very special date'
She brings a range of garments, every colour shape and style,
Then 'How is Modom doing?' she asks me with a smile . . .

Well . . .

'The thing wrong with the two piece is the wool clings to my thighs,
And . . . well . . . all things considered, this comes as no surprise.
The cat-suit would look lovely . . . if I lost a lot of weight
And the trousers would fit like a dream, if I were five foot eight,
But since I'm only five foot two, they really are no good . . .
Unless you've got designer stilts in a matching shade of wood?
I really liked the lycra, and the colour's me, it's true
But it did impair my breathing and my lips went rather blue.
I fear the jersey body was too tight around the crutch
And that throttled look around the neck did bother me a touch.
The drop-waist dress was pretty, but what really puzzled me
Was why the drop-waist, in my case, came way below the knee?
Now, the fluffy green angora was a really perfect length
But on me its comic element would be its only strength.
The beaded glitzy evening dress, full length and slit to thigh
Was an interesting choice of yours, I really can't deny,
And though I really take your point re matching shoes and bag
I doubt if they would make me look less like a man in drag.
The power suit was stunning and had only one real flaw;
You'd never get those shoulder pads through any normal door.
And the cocktail dress was sexy, really showed my cleavage off,
But I feel things could get tricky if I had to sneeze or cough.
And finally, the crêpe de Chine might well have looked quite svelte . . .
But underneath the armpits is an odd place for a belt.

Well, I think that's almost everything, you've really done your best
It's not your fault I'm short and plump with a very ample chest!
It's not your fault most clothes are made with a slim size eight in
   mind
And rarely take into account short legs and a big behind.'

I change into my leggings, and my lovely baggy top.
I think I'll try mail order, next time I have to shop.

I Haven't a Thing to Wear

It's New Year's Eve. Eight forty-five.
And what was mere despair
Has turned into hysteria . . .
I HAVEN'T A THING TO WEAR!

Discarded clothes are strewn around,
We're due to leave at nine;
But something tells me I may not
Be ready quite on time!

There seems no clear solution
To this most disastrous plight;
Those few clothes that were suitable
Are all post-Christmas TIGHT!

My husband shows no sympathy.
Can't share the angst I feel.
He says 'he's heard it all before'
But this time IT'S FOR REAL!

He starts to pick out garments
(I sense this is unwise)
Each time he asks 'What's wrong with this?'
I hiss 'It's not my size!'

We've been through all my impulse buys
Now he's found my BIG MISTAKE
When he holds out the Ra Ra skirt
It's more than I can take.

And then I have a great idea
A ruse that will impress;
I'll wear that skirt and say I thought
That it was fancy dress!

It's a Cover-Up

A girl's best friend?
Without a doubt
The baggy jumper wins.
Voluminously covering
A multitude of sins.
The virtues of this garment
I will long and loudly preach,
Enveloping extremities
Most others cannot reach.
So if things do get out of hand
Grow over large, get saggy . . .
Forget the clingy and well cut;
You can't go wrong with baggy.

P.S.

Elasticated waistbands
Cannot go without a mention
To have no buttons, belts or zips
Relieves a lot of tension.

Going for a Thong

Some people must believe
That they look sexy
In a
Thong.

I have to say that
Ninety-nine percent of them
Are
Wrong.

It's in the Jeans

There's no two ways about it
Someone has shrunk these jeans
I've hardly got them past my thighs
And they're straining at the seams.
I'll have to get them on somehow
And stretch them back to size,
But the task is not an easy one
And brings tears to my eyes.
There's quite a large expanse of flesh
Where two zip parts should meet
(A lesser woman than myself
Would now admit defeat)
It's just mind over matter
As I shift myself about
(Though I really wish my navel
Would not keep on popping out!)
To facilitate the process
I lie flat on the ground
And, grappling madly with the zip,
Emit strange grunting sounds.
I thrash around for quite some time
Until success at last . . .
But I know well from experience
The danger has not passed,
Now for the really tricky part
To get up off the floor,
For whatever hasn't gone all numb
Is feeling really sore.
I try to raise my torso
Then I try to move a limb,

Though the odds on getting vertical
Are looking pretty slim.
But after lots of writhing
The denim seems less tight,
I roll and heave and stretch and bend
And find myself upright . . .
I limber up, I touch my toes
And then jog on the spot,
Though working out in denim jeans
Does make you feel so hot.
I must look like a mummy
(The embalmed Egyptian sort)
Who, though bound up quite tightly
Does so love the odd cavort.
Well now that I've achieved my goal
I really need a break . . .
But opting for the easy chair
Was a really big mistake;
Yes, lowering my weary form
Was when I made my blunder . . .
The strain was too much for my jeans
That zip just tore asunder.
Well, at least a lesson has been learned,
And on one thing I'm insistent . . .
Next time I shop for denims,
I'll make sure they're shrink resistant.

Relative Values

New Man

The 'New Man' he is sensitive, he's caring and he's kind,
He has respect for women, understands the female mind.
He'll never crack a sexist joke, or ogle at page three
And words like tart and crumpet only crop up over tea.
At home he does not think in terms of 'jobs that women do'
He'll change the baby's nappy (even if it's done a poo.)
He'll gladly do the shopping, don the apron, wield the pan;
He has no need to prove that he is Mr Macho Man.
The thing is, he is hard to find and it will be sod's law
That if you come across one, he is always spoken for.

If New Man's not how you'd describe your partner or your spouse,
Who's baffled by the concepts 'shared child-care' and 'help round
     house'
Please don't despair, it's not too late for his re-education,
Though you'll need patience, nerves of steel and a lot of
     dedication.
Results will not come overnight, the struggle may be long,
'A leopard cannot change its spots' he'll cry, but you'll say 'WRONG'
He'll need some strong convincing, and dear sisters, here's the rub;
When faced with earnest reasoning, he'll leg it to the pub.
But don't give up the battle, for inside that lazy lout
There may just be a New Man simply dying to get out.

As wistfully we shake our heads, and breathe a weary sigh,
We gaze up at that herd of pigs that's sailing through the sky.

I Lost my Man to a Microchip or . . .
I'd Prefer a Nibble to a Byte!

He reads computer magazines . . . well, fine
But now I feel I must voice my complaint;
For everything there is a place and time
But frankly, bedtime reading, they just ain't!
Seductively I whisper in his ear
But quickly sense that I'm on to a loser,
When he replies, 'Please don't disturb me, dear . . .
I'm only half way through my *PC User*.'
Without a doubt this wealth of magazines
Has kept him up to date with high-tech fashion,
I wouldn't really mind except it seems
They very rarely lead to nights of passion.
One night I said, 'Look! Here's the *Karma Sutra*!'
He said, 'I'll read it after *What Computer*.'

One Thing at a Time

How did they come to be that singleminded.
Just one thing at a time is most men's way.
The task at hand and to all else they're blinded.
It drives some women mad, I'm bound to say.

While women carry out their routine juggling –
Six jobs at once without a second thought,
The very concept would leave most men struggling;
Child sit AND make the tea would leave them fraught.

What is it like reclining in the armchair
Oblivious to all . . . stone deaf to sound?
He's deep in the newspaper and quite unaware
Of dramas now unfolding all around.

When you entrust some fathers with the child care
On your return you'll feel a sense of dread;
It's justified! The house will be a nightmare,
The kids will be unhinged, unbathed, unfed.

In the thick-pile there's a crisp and biscuit hotchpotch
Someone has re-upholstered your new suite
There's a friendly Martian busy watching *Baywatch*
And your man? Behind the paper. Fast asleep.

A strange phenomenon, but so apparent,
But tell me where's the reason, where's the rhyme?
Just how did men acquire that special talent
Of doing only one thing at a time?

Stupor Woman

It is hard to feel mellow and sexy
Or have amorous thoughts on your mind
With brain numb and bones weary
Eyes bloodshot and bleary
At the end of a day's heavy grind.

When your children have bickered and bellowed
And a burst pipe left your kitchen flooded,
It is fair to assume
When you hit the bedroom
That you may not feel all that hot-blooded.

And it's hardly surprising in fairness
That those thoughts of wild passion are few,
When you've spent quite a while
On the brand new thick pile
Extricating a chewed rusk or two.

You must somehow convey to your partner
His libido tonight must be curbed
For your tired aching bones
And erogenous zones
Would be much rather left undisturbed.

In response to his meaningful winking
And the nudge in the ribs, oh so tender,
It does seem somewhat tough
To impart the rebuff;
'Hanky Panky's not on the agenda.'

Though some nights you are driven by ardour
And your passions run terribly deep,
There are days like today
When there's really no way
Bed means anything other than sleep.

And although you do wish things were different
You conclude with a sense of regret,
That tonight you just know
Some crunch creams and cocoa
Are as wicked as you're going to get.

These Foolish Things Remind Me of You

with apologies to Holt Marvell

The way you fling your dirty socks across the bedroom.
The way for months on end you say 'I'll fix that drain soon'
The seat left up in the loo.
These foolish things remind me of you.

The way you quickly scarper when I do the dishes.
The way you wear those flares against my deepest wishes.
The way you snore . . . yes it's true
These foolish things remind me of you.

You came . . . you saw . . . you conquered me
And when you did that to me
Had no idea what your 'habits' might be.

The way you still have not grasped how to use the oven.
The way you call my closest friends 'The Witches Coven'
The trailed toothpaste, spilled shampoo.
These foolish things remind me of you.

The way your very first grey hair was so traumatic.
The way you find apologising problematic.
The way you sneeze and it's flu.
These foolish things remind me of you.

You came . . . You saw . . . You conquered me.
And when you did that to me
I knew not what your strange ways might be

The way you tell me when I've got premenstrual tension.
The way your bald patch is the thing one must not mention.
The way you think you're in tune.
These foolish things remind me of you.

The way you tell me when to change gear when I'm driving.
The way you always go out as my mum's arriving.
These foolish things . . . strange but true
In spite of all this . . . I wouldn't swap you.

Males on Wheels

When helping out the spouse with navigation
It's strange how thoughts can oft turn to divorce;
The journey ends in pure exasperation,
He'll lose his temper, it's par for the course.
Whenever I'm map reading I have found
He can't refrain from constant criticising,
He yells 'The bloody map's the wrong way round!'
I hiss, 'You make me tense. it's not surprising
We're lost!' And now he'll loose his cool completely.
He'll really rant and rave with all his might,
'Why can't you just stay calm?' I ask him sweetly.
He screams, 'Why can't you tell your left from right?'
So next time he suggests I navigate
I'll bear in mind . . . I may just need Relate.

Distress of the Poetess

I'm sure that Shakespeare never had to stop
In mid creative flow of play or sonnet
To write a list and do the weekly shop
On Stratford High Street. I would bet upon it.
It's true of most great men of poetry
Quite unencumbered by domestic matters;
For them no cry of 'Dad, I need a wee!'
Which leaves that half-formed couplet all in tatters.
I lock myself away and I aspire
To lofty thoughts but all quite fruitlessly.
I scan the page, the spirit's soared no higher
Than . . . Defrost fridge. Name tapes. Spag bol for tea.
Oh lucky men, you've no idea how hard
It is to be a housewife, mum and bard.

They Are Not With Me

The commuter train to Paddington is crammed with city types,
All reading their *Financial Times* and dressed in smart pin-stripes.
And here am I with my two boys aged nearly five and three,
And I've briefed them on behaving well and talking quietly.
We've not been there two minutes when I stiffen as I hear
The loudest 'whisper' ever heard directed at my ear,
'You see that man with the funny hair! Those fluffy bits look silly'
Then follows, as an afterthought, 'And I bet he's got a willy.'
From behind a dozen papers, gentle titters can be heard.
(Perhaps I should pretend to faint, is the first thought that
    occurred.)
Our travelling companion, red haired and now red faced,
Accepts the mumbled grovel from a mother who's disgraced.
I hiss a little lecture that is fitting to the crime,
And wonder if I should announce that 'really, they're not mine!'
No time, for they are off again; I wince as I hear, 'Mummy
Just how *did* Daddy get my seed to go inside your tummy?'
I sense a sudden stillness, not a single sound is heard
The scanning of the stocks and shares momentarily deferred.
They are waiting for my answer and all eyes are now on me.
(Why do I get the feeling they enjoy my agony?)
Well, do call me old fashioned but I feel I must confess
I wouldn't choose this topic for the Paddington Express.
But older brother saves the day with his worldly explanation
(As I contemplate alighting – on my own – at the next station)
'Dad keeps seeds in his willy; when he wants to make one grow
He pokes her belly button. I watched, that's how I know'
This seems a timely moment to drop a magazine,
I dive down to retrieve it, where I sweat and blush unseen.
I rummage with conviction for as long as I am able

Till one of them yells, 'Mummy, don't hide underneath the table!'
I finally emerge composed and note that my two boys
Are now all innocence and charm and busy with their toys.
My pin-striped train companions read their *FT*'s as before
'Let the train take the strain' the slogan goes,
But somehow I'm not sure . . .

The House of the Rising Sons

There is a house in Gloucestershire –
You'll know it from the noise –
Where pre-school dramas rend the air
Starring me and my two boys.

Each day there'll be a different theme . . .
A brand new plot unfolds,
That sorely tries the patience
Of this mother's heart of gold.

Some days you'll hear the odd cross word
Some days a witch-like scream.
It's variable, my 'stress response'
Twixt 7 and 8.15

Plot A. Sweatshirt scenario:
All nicely clean and pressed
Then a Weetabix-type incident
Means . . . well . . . you guess the rest.

While frantic search ensues to find
A clean one, you just know
That severely-cereal-splattered son
Will claim, 'It doesn't show'

Plot B. Son number two has news:
A packed lunch! WHAT! TODAY?
Well since it's ten past eight, my sweet,
Will dry bread be okay?

This has reminded number one
At 8.14 to boot . . .
'Oh yes . . . It's harvest festival,
I need tins, flowers and fruit . . .'

How to describe emotions
Aroused by what I hear?
Hysterical-type explosion
I suppose comes fairly near.

It all comes to a sudden head
With a high-pitched screamed admission,
'I AM JUST A NORMAL MOTHER
NOT A MIND-READER OR MAGICIAN!'

We leave the house. *En route* for school
A murmur comes my way
'I hope you packed my football kit
We've got a match today.'

Why do my knuckles look so white
Upon the steering wheel?
And two words 'boarding school'
Now seem to have immense appeal.

Down to Earth

In midst of Shirley Valentine-esque dream
As swarthy Greek declares his love anew
I'm cruelly interrupted by a scream
Of 'Come quick, mum, I think I've done a poo'.
Reality has reared its cruel head
My Grecian God has disappeared from sight;
I drag my shell-shocked form out of the bed
To help my offspring in his tricky plight.

Engrossed in gripping read of hate and greed;
(He's going to kill her, tension's very high.)
I vaguely hear a 'Mummy, quick, I need
A heavy axe; The baddie's going to die.'
'Okay, my sweet, you'll find one in the shed'
I murmur faintly from my paperback.
AN AXE! The words form coldly in my head.
Am I too late to stop this crazed attack?

I'm sipping on a cool drink in the sun,
I'm almost on that balmy, golden beach,
I'm restful, calm and feeling 'all at one'
When suddenly I hear a high-pitched screech.
Slight pause, and then a 'Right I'm telling mum'
I brace myself for tears, recrimination,
My mood of relaxation quite undone
By unmaternal thoughts and deep frustration.

No time for mental transports of delight,
No point in dreams or idle reverie . . .
You've got to be on call, your children might
Require a weapon, wipe or referee.

Presumed Innocent

Off with young son for meeting
With headmaster of new school.
Though only four and 'seven mumfs'
This boy is no one's fool.
And when I say 'Please do behave'
He rolls his eyes at me,
'Don't worry, Mum, I won't say words
Like willy, poo or wee.'
Somewhat relieved to know at least
We seem to have this straight,
But suffer set-back as he yells
'New school, Can't bloody wait!'

Our interview goes smoothly
Well, as far as one can tell.
My son is bright and chirpy
(And I'm trying hard as well)
He chats about his pets and friends
His toys, the family;
'My Mum's quite old, she's firty-eight,
My bruvver's only free!'
At last shake hands politely
And we're heading for the door,
When pride and joy decides he wants
To add a snippet more . . .

And looking back, that old cliché,
So near and yet so far,
In one more minute we'd have both
Been safely in the car.
I hear my son's angelic voice
And freeze in disbelief . . .
'You know my mum,
Well her bum wobbles
When she brushes teef!'
Head doesn't even bat an eye
He's blessed with chivalry.
His look just says 'boys will be boys,
And your secret's safe with me.'

Can't help but wonder when paths cross
On parents' nights to come,
If he will look at me and think;
'Ah yes, the wobbly bum!'

Tales from the Domestic Front

I Put it Somewhere Safe

Our holiday is imminent
But I am in despair
I've put the passports somewhere safe
But I can't remember where.
I put them somewhere sensible
Where they won't be disturbed
And no doubt ever seen again
(No wonder I'm perturbed!)
I've checked all normal places
The ones I'd tend to use
To keep all vital documents
That I don't want to lose.
The desk drawer in the study
The cupboard by my bed . . .
I must have had a brainwave . . .
Picked a 'safer place' instead.
Some lateral thinking is required
To save me from this mess
(I feel the panic rising
And other signs of stress.)
My family is unaware
Of what might be our fate
(And barely bats an eyelid
As I hyper-ventilate.)
I'll have to break the news to them
Express my deep remorse
(My children will disown me
And he'll file for divorce.)
But suddenly I get a grip
Just in the nick of time;

I tell myself to 'just keep calm
And all will turn out fine.'
A plan of action is required
A search that's systematic
(And this said by a woman who
Is chronically erratic.)
The search is on in earnest
And with a flash of inspiration
Decide the bathroom cabinet
Is worth investigation.
I've always found it useful
As a handy little 'nook' . . .
And so with heartbeat pounding
I proceed to take a look.
It looks as though I've used it as
A 'pending-tray' of late
My pot of bronzing moisture cream
Is now a paper-weight.
Between my light-hold styling-mousse
And my evening primrose pills
I find a few bank statements
And Oh God, some unpaid bills.
But sadly passports, there are none
The search must move elsewhere
I'll try the kitchen dresser
For who knows? They might be there.
It's crammed with toys and cook books,
Letters, plasters, bits of string,
(It's just that sort of handy place
Where I put . . . everything.)
And though I'm really chuffed to find
My *Best of Wham* cassette
The fact the passports are not there
Does cause me deep regret.

Now I can think of one more place
That's maybe worth a try,
If they're not here, it looks as though
It's holiday bye-bye.
I have a little rummage
And to my great surprise
A little pile of passports
Just appears before my eyes.
I'm overwhelmed with great relief
My joy is unsurpassed . . .
It's Gatwick Airport here we come
And sun and sea at last.
If only I had thought this through
And looked in here before . . .
It's obvious I'd keep them . . . .
In my tights and knicker drawer.

Ode to Her with Flair

How I wish I had your talent
For interior design.
With no hint of any effort
The result is quite divine.
Just the way you scatter cushions,
Fling a throw across a chair,
Place some nick-nacks on a table,
Just admit it . . . you've got flair.
It's no wonder I stand back in awe
And yield a heavy sigh,
For regrettably, it would appear
This flair thing's passed me by.

As I plump my Snoopy cushions
On my 'leather-look' *chaise-longue*
I am forced to ask the question
Just where am I going wrong?
Are the gold silk drapes too gaudy?
Were mink walls my big mistake?
Would the tiger rug work better
If it looked less like a fake?
Is the chandelier too glitzy
For my humble little home?
Should I move the cupid statue
Outside . . . closer to the gnome?

Well I asked for your opinion
For advice on what to do
But the last thing I expected was,
'There's just no hope for you!'
Yes, I noticed how you rolled your eyes
And sadly shook your head,
Where I'd hoped for help and guidance
I got sympathy instead.
And your one 'constructive' comment
Was insensitive and trite,
'For immediate improvement
I'd severely dim the light.'

So I thanked you for your expertise
And sent you on your way,
Who would want to be in
Bloody *Country Living*
Anyway?

Maybe I Should Have Gone to Finishing School After All

I cannot crochet booties, nor have I mastered smocking
My few attempts at knitting have really been quite shocking
I cannot follow patterns so that rules out making clothes
I cannot even sew a hem, though I do try, heaven knows.
I've never run up curtains or upholstered any suite,
My one attempt at making blinds soon ended in defeat.
I never cracked embroidery or for that matter quilting,
If I arrange fresh flowers, well they always end up wilting.
I really fare no better at attempts at *haute cuisine*
My gastronomic efforts are far from a gourmet's dream . . .
My cakes are either very flat or soggy in the middle . . .
How others make their soufflés rise is something of a riddle.
I haven't really got much flair for interior design,
No chance of *Homes and Gardens* doing any room of mine.
They'd take one look around *chez moi* and dismiss it at a glance,
Not appreciative of chaos in a 'homely' ambience.
And then of course there's D.I.Y. it's not my greatest skill;
I would be good at painting but the smell makes me quite ill.
Wallpaper, with one look from me, just slides right off the wall,
I had a stab at woodwork but with no success at all!
I've tried my hand with bathroom tiles, but they always seem to break
I volunteered for grouting once; this was a big mistake!
And then of course, electrics . . . no real need here to expand
But DANGER is the word I'd use were I to lend a hand.
So my domestic talents are few and far between . . .
I should have gone to finishing school as can be clearly seen.
But what if I could do all this, when would I find the time
To lounge around at home all day and think of words that rhyme?

Be Prepared

For some efficient types I know, well nothing could be easier
Than making sure they've always got a very well-stocked freezer.
They know if unexpected guests should show up day or night
They can say with total confidence, 'You must stay for a bite'.
There'll be a home-made pie or two, some soup, a cake, a
   stew . . .
And pop it in the microwave is all they'll have to do.
Their larder will be brimming with the kinds of things you spy
In those very fancy deli's . . . but you'd never ever buy;
The sauces and the marinades, six different types of rice,
Oriental things in tins and jars of most exotic spice.
Their fridge will yield fresh pasta, pesto sauce and things in brine
Sun-dried tomatoes soaked in oil, and of course some chilled white
   wine.
There'll be a good French cheese or two, some salami, and pâté
And a choice of salad leaves (and vinaigrettes, needless to say!)
And finally some nice fresh herbs, coriander, thyme and dill
Can just be plucked from little pots along the window sill.
They will fling all this together and in the twinkle of an eye
A gastronomic feast appears for those who just dropped by.

But if quite unexpectedly you dropped in to *chez-nous*
Let's take a look to see what I might have in store for you . . .
The freezer's always worth a try, and yields the odd surprise . . .
And yes I've found some ice-pops and a big bag of French fries!
And you just can't beat fish fingers for a quick and easy meal,
I could always do them *gratinée* depending how you feel.
And what is this right at the back ? I've seen that tub before . . .
It's labelled 'puréed baby food' That baby is now four!
Well let's now try the larder, take a look to see what's there . . .

49

(Though that Mother Hubbard feeling tells me I will find it bare)
Well, here's a tin of best baked beans, we can split it if you're
   willing . . .
Or what about these Taco Shells, though sorry . . . I've no filling.
There's a packet of Basmati Rice, with some sauce it would be
   fine
I can just make out the sell-by date . . . October '89.
And finally I'll check the fridge though I'm mortified to say
My last sun-dried tomatoes all got used up yesterday.
Apart from that, there's a pack of lard, one egg, a sausage roll,
And I cannot quite identify what's in the little bowl.

So to all potential visitors, there's one thing I would say;
If you're planning to surprise me, do please bring a take-away.

Always Read the Recipe Right to the Very End

Always read the recipe right to the very end,
I speak from long experience and advise you as a friend;
For often in my cooking I've been carried quite away
Busy knocking up some *haute cuisine* in a gay abandoned way,
But as I smugly finish off and think I'm quite a cook
I idly scan the recipe and take one final look,
And then I see those vital words I somehow missed first time
(Which is why my cooking's always more sub-standard than
    sublime.)
I recall a certain soufflé, when alas, too late, I found
I added all the walnuts whole instead of finely ground.
And the time I beat a dozen eggs, if only I had waited
Till I'd read the next line where I saw that key word . . . separated.
And yes, that piquant bubbling sauce, the fruit of one hour's toil
How did I miss that heavy type, 'Do not allow to boil!'
Once, cake inside the oven, it was then I learnt the worst . . .
My eye was caught by that crucial phrase 'Preheat the oven first'
And about to serve that sumptuous dish, I check I've got it right
I spot the tip hitherto unseen, 'Marinate it overnight.'
Yet the time when I was well prepared and cooked the night
    before
The three words, 'Serve at once' somehow were the three I never
    saw.
So please do heed my warning, and never skip a line . . .
You'll save yourself ingredients, embarrassment and time.

Fridge Over Troubled Water

When life just gets on top of me
My fridge, without a doubt,
Can offer consolation
It's the place to . . . just chill out.

And when I cannot take the heat
And troubles just abound,
I simply open up that door
And have a graze around.

A dip in here, a slice from there,
No morsel should be spurned,
Variety is everything
No jar is left unturned.

Yes comfort eating's where it's at
When life and friends are fickle;
I find a pound of nice chilled cheese
Can help – with ploughman's pickle.

Leftovers can be calming
And I find that, as a rule,
To polish off a Sunday joint
Can help me keep my cool.

Yes 'fridgeing' gives great solace
And never should be knocked.
(Remember though it will not work
Unless it's kept well stocked!)

Let us Now Praise Famous Spreads

Most great institutions will be eulogised
And such tributes are fitting and right,
But I must say that I am extremely suprised
Very little's been writ on Marmite!

Fatal Attraction

Behold that perfect vision of a fresh chocolate éclair,
Whose squidgy, gooey gorgeousness is just beyond compare.
It's high up on the 'blissful' scale – it's in a world apart;
A Danish, say comes nowhere near, nor does a custard tart.
Don't try to show resistance faced with this patisserie;
Succumb to the temptation; be seduced . . . deliciously.
No don't hold back! Indulge! Cast out all thoughts of guilt or sin,
Life's too short for abstention! Do not let the diet win.
For a bit of what you fancy, as they say, is good for you.
Just be careful not to bite off any more than you can choux.

The Carnivore is Over

with apologies to The Seekers

Say good-bye to chops and spare-ribs,
Lamb hot-pot
And Shepherds Pie,
Though it breaks my heart to do this
I'm afraid
It's meat bye-bye.

Say hello to well-soaked lentils
Mixed nut roasts
And veggie-bake.
Those chick peas caused me huge problems.
I bought tofu . . .
Big mistake.

Like a drum my heart is beating
I smell bacon being fried.
Can I overcome these longings?
Can my cravings be denied?

In a mirage I see roast beef
But such thoughts
I must control;
What about the moral issue
And the high
Cholesterol?

Like a drum, my heart is beating,
Neighbours with their barbecue.
How I yearn for something meaty
Just a little steak would do.

Started out with good intentions
But now must admit defeat,
Since for me
There's no escaping
Those two veg
Cry out for meat.

Just Desserts

Dessert. Some pass. They're 'trying to be good'
But I've no time for virtuous pretences;
I cry 'I'll have the sticky toffee pud
With fudge ice-cream . . . and hang the consequences.'
Life's far too short for boring self-control
Or choosing lesser evils like sorbet,
I say 'Bring on life's heaving trifle bowl
And take that healthy fruit salad away!'
My friend has fresh pineapple. How terrific!
(She's petrified of putting on an ounce)
Not me, I want the highly calorific . . .
'Gâteau . . . with cream . . .' I brazenly announce
My friend whines; 'You'll get fat' (She's such a riot!)
But I say 'Vive Le Pud . . . and stuff the diet!'

Trials and Tribulations

Update on the Girl from Ipanema

Young and tanned
And slim and lovely
The girl from Ipanema goes walking
And as she passes
Each woman she passes
Goes ggrrrrrrrr.

I'm Sick of Supermodels

I'm sick of supermodels
And the time has come, I fear,
To say, in no uncertain terms
Saturation point is here.
Be it pictures of the catwalk
As they coolly strut their stuff,
Or the covers of the glossies . . .
I've really had enough.
On the hoardings, in the papers,
In the adverts on TV
Yes she who models is indeed
A big celebrity.
They are even on the chat shows
Being interviewed of late,
No, there's no escaping Linda
Naomi, Claudia or Kate.
And it's double strength exposure
In the media today;
They don't just bare their bodies
But they also have their say;
'I'm an ordinary person
Just like the girl next door . . .
Except I live with a rock star
And earn a fraction more.'
And amazing revelations
That just take one's breath away,
Like 'I'm happiest when wearing jeans'
Or, 'I phone home every day.'
And, 'At home I wear no make up,
Just some liner round my eyes

And perhaps a touch of lip gloss
BUT I ALWAYS MOISTURIZE.'
I do not want their health tips
And I know this might offend
But 'supermodel's beauty secrets'
Drive me round the bend.
I couldn't give a damn about
How they control their weight,
The massive fees that they command
Or the pop stars that they date.
They won't get out of bed for less
Than fifteen grand a day,
But frankly I'd be happier
If bed is where they'd stay.
I'm tired of perfect bodies
And legs that stretch for miles,
I'm tired of paparazzi shots
All teeth and hair and smiles.
To the over-exposed and overpaid
This suggestion I would make:
'Why not take early retirement
And give us all a break!'

Ode of Moral Support to a Friend on Reaching Forty

Dear friend, please do not be forlorn,
For you are not that old
You don't look more than thirty-nine
If I may be so bold!
So don't approach this milestone
With great horror and deep dread
Think 'life begins at forty' type of
Cheerful thoughts instead.
I say 'ignore time's ravages
Those little tell-tale signs'
I cry, 'those are not wrinkles . . .
They are just your laughter lines.'
I shriek, 'don't hark back to your youth
Don't think the future's bleak . . .
The fortysomething woman
Is a woman at her peak.'
And if this fails to lift your gloom
One final tip I proffer;
They're selling anti-ageing cream
At Boots . . . on special offer.

Infernal Internal

Your routine check-up – yet somehow
Those words fill you with dread,
'Remove your tights and panties
And just hop up on the bed.'

You try to feel at ease yet
Muscles tighten as you're told,
'You've seen this many times before . . .
I hope it's not too cold.'

Ah yes, the trusty speculum
Ooh yes, we know it well . . .
This does not stop it looking like
Some torture out of hell.

Your doctor disappears from view
Somewhere inside your skirt
From where you'll hear the muffled words,
' Relax, this will not hurt.'

And, in all truth, it's not so bad
And over in a flash.
One hurdle left: put pants back on
With dignity, panache.

Okay, it's not a fun day out;
Undignified? Yes true.
But now and then we women
'Gotta do
What we gotta do!'

The Wrinkle Cream Blues

I'd like to take you back in time, to not that long ago
When a little dab of face cream gave our skin its youthful glow.
Were we obsessed with wrinkles then? Did crow's feet make us
    fraught
In the age before a wrinkle-free existence could be bought?
But those wrinkles are big business, there's an industry out there
Spending billions just to tell us to invest in good skin-care;
And they tell us how they test, concoct, research with great furore
Till they come up with the cream to keep us young for evermore.
And gradually we start to think that maybe it is true . . .
And that we'll be amazed at what a pot of cream can do.
I scan cosmetic counters and the women's magazines
But the secret of eternal youth is harder than it seems.
It is very scientific with a strange vocabulary
(Which would no doubt pose no problem if you're good at
    chemistry.)
There is elastine and collagen, lipisomes and ceramides,
There are alpha hydroxide acids, and what the French call
    'anti-rides'.
There is oil free, and there's fragrance free and hypo-allergenic
And there's also Ph balanced and there's non-comedogenic.
There are special creams for eyes and necks, for morning and for
    night
(And no doubt for in-between times there's a cream to see you
    right.)
And then if you're feeling prune-like, or you get a sudden urge
For some serious hydration, then there's always 'moisture surge'.
If your skin is dry or oily, normal, even combination
Dermatologically speaking, there's a perfect preparation.
They rejuvenate, replenish, they refresh . . . revitalize,

And other words that start with R . . . before your very eyes.
And if diagrams are up your street, you'll really have a ball
(Those that show you 'cell renewal' I feel really top 'em all.)
But I find this glut of face-cream speak is all too much for me . . .
(What I need is an interpreter . . . to grow old gracefully.)
And then, suppose I make my choice, it's a very costly job;
For this wrinkle-free existence costs you FIFTY PENCE A BLOB!
I'm quite aware my face reveals that I am past my prime,
And of course I could do more to stop the ravages of time,
But now, heading for my forties, I am finally aware
That one's beauty comes from deep within . . . not just from good
   skin care.
So I'm sticking with the cream I've got, though its way behind the
   times
Incidentally, mine aren't wrinkles . . . no . . .
They are my laughter lines.

A Woman's Lot

A woman's lot in many ways is not an easy one.
Yes, it's great to be a woman, but it isn't always fun.
There's the menstrual cycle for a start, a vital function true;
But those thirty years of P.M.T., can take their toll on you.
Violent mood swings are not funny, peace and calm are cast aside;
Without warning Dr Jekyll can turn into Mrs Hyde!
Then the tiredness and the stomach cramps, sore beasts, water
   retention
And those 'other irritations' that one doesn't like to mention.
And no sooner than you're through with this, you've reached the
   menopause.
I would say that being female, if I'm honest, has its flaws.
Then of course the ageing process, time is very rarely kind,
And those wrinkly, saggy, flabby bits are something of a bind.
But, if all this sounds too gloomy, just remember if you can . . .
That things could have been a great deal worse . . .
You could have been a MAN!

The Power of Advertising

They say that things can happen when you have a Badedas Bath
That you can really count on a romantic aftermath
So having tipped the bottle in, I soak luxuriously
Anticipating all the while what lies in store for me.
Then towel wrapped around me . . . sorry . . . draped seductively,
I wait at the bathroom window . . . just as seen on my TV.
But nothing is occurring, no horse, no man in sight
(I check the empty bottle to make sure I did it right)
The minutes pass, I'm shivering, no suitor I behold . . .
What happens after a Badedas bath . . . is you catch a bloody cold.

They say romance will surely come to those that drink Gold Blend
You'll meet a handsome neighbour and who knows how it will
    end?
Well, anything is worth a try so I make myself a cup
And hark I hear the doorbell ring and hastily jump up;
That Gold Blend really works a treat, tonight will be the night.
I throw the door wide open, to welcome Mr Right;
But things are not quite as I planned as I hear my caller speak,
'There's water flooding in downstairs . . . I think you've got a leak!'
Not an ounce of romance in him, the rotten, whinging louse,
You can keep your jar of Gold Blend . . . I'll stick with Maxwell
    House.

They say that there's adventure for the girl that likes Milk Tray . . .
That fearless, strong and handsome men just cannot keep away.
They'll go to any lengths at all, there's nothing they won't do
To make sure of delivering that half pound box to you.
Well tonight's a sort of 'milk tray night', I can feel it in the air
As I slip on something slinky, apply lip gloss and toss hair . . .

Then, munching through some current stock, I lounge, all charm
   and poise
Ears straining for 'a leap from helicopter' sort of noise.
But I'm down to my last orange cream, and I hear no 'action'
   sounds . . .
Tomorrow I'll be spotty and have gained at least three pounds.

I drank that awful Cointreau, but no Frenchman came my way
I tried the cereal squirrels love . . . even they stayed right away
It was then I really saw the light, yes it all seemed clear to me . . .
I should give up watching adverts . . . and switch on to BBC!

Book at Beach Time

The airport bookshop. Time to make a choice.
This holiday I want something highbrow.
'You must be joking' says the inner voice,
'Why change the habit of a lifetime now?'
It's true. My taste in books does tend towards light.
So with all the conviction I can muster,
I search out books to make me erudite.
(Ignoring large display marked 'New Bonkbuster')
I know I need the mental stimulation,
A spot of intellectual cut and thrust,
Yet such books sadly lack that combination
Of power, greed, debauchery and lust.
But wait . . . must think ahead . . . to sun-soaked stupor.
I'll stop this farce . . . and buy the Jilly Cooper.

I'm Only Here for the Bore

The hostess promised company with charm and wit galore,
But I'm stuck in a corner with a really dreadful bore.
I try to show some interest as he gleefully explains
That since the age of six he's had a passion for . . . steam trains.
He's rattling on at quite a pace, I've had it now, methinks,
I wonder if he'd notice if I just had forty winks.
I wish I had the guts to say 'I hope that you don't mind
I'm off to find some charm and wit . . . I'm not the steam train
   kind!'

My next encounter starts so well, she's charming as can be,
But soon it is apparent that she wants to talk to me
About her son 'the genius' who walks and talks and writes,
And does impersonations, and sleeps right through the night.
He eats well, and is potty trained and does what he is told . . .
Now isn't that amazing for a child of ten months old?
I wish I had the nerve to say, 'Shut up a minute, you!
If we're talking "brilliant offspring" well, you ought to meet my
   two!'

And finally, there's one last chance, the night is drawing on,
Just one more brief encounter . . . and then I must be gone.
My hostess introduces me to a man who's 'just amazing'
So how come he is prattling on about his double glazing?
He's built a new conservatory, it's turned out such a treat . . .
'You just can't beat those windows for the way they keep in heat.'
I wish that I could tell him; 'D.I.Y. just leaves me cold . . .
And you could bore for England, dear, if I may be so bold.'

Well so much for the wit and charm that never came my way
It's time to make my exit, call this endless night a day.
Three hours ago this very room seemed really quite inviting . . .
But frankly, watching *Neighbours* would have been much more
exciting.

Tunnel Vision

Exciting times for those that love La France;
Pour le voyage, a quicker way by far.
But I won't use that tunnel, not a chance.
Me ride Le Shuttle? *Absolument pas!*
Perhaps it is my nervous disposition
That makes me want to cry out '*Sacré Bleu!*'
Just thinking of myself in that position
Beneath the English Channel! *Quel horreur!*
Call me old fashioned but I feel the ferry
Will serve me well as it has always done.
I told the travel agent, '*Ecoute cheri,*
I just do not use tunnels, *tu comprends?*'
I have to say that my *bêtes-noires* are few . . .
But deep-sea drama? *Non, merci beaucoup!*'

Weathering the Forecast

I know you weathermen all know your stuff
And like to share your knowledge of our climes,
But frankly I feel I have had enough
Of arrows, charts, and endless curvy lines.
'Atlantic frontal systems', leave me cold
As does all talk of 'ridges of depression',
'Tight isobars' mean wind, we're always told,
But why not say the word . . . without digression?
Those 'radar rainfall' routines are a bore,
As are blurred pictures from the satellite,
And yet with all these aids one can't ignore
You still can't get those 'weather fronts' quite right.
So don't blind us with science, cease this folly;
Just tell us – plainly – will we need a brolly?

The Festive Season

The Festive Season

Oh to be in England
Now that August's here
Especially if you're into
Very early Christmas cheer.
The bucket and the spades
Have only just been put away
And lo! the Christmas Catalogues
Arrive by post each day.

September comes, and you will find
That almost every store
Is busy clearing out its shelves
For Chistmas gifts galore.
So for efficient types and
Forward planners, there's the chance
To get that Christmas shopping done
Some four months in advance.

October. No escaping
That the festive season's here
With eighty shopping days to go
The big day's getting near.
So I bought the chocolate novelties
For the tree, but have to say
That I wasn't sure that they would last
So I ate them . . . that same day.

November. TV adverts
Morn and night . . . we're saturated.
The children's lists are being compiled
And constantly updated.
The Christmas overkill again
Ignore it all I say
Too soon for Christmas shopping . . .
It's still six weeks away.

December. Time is running out
That shopping will not wait.
The panic sets in very fast . . .
I've left it much too late.
Now the big day's round the corner
One thing really gets me hopping;
I've had five months and look at me . . .
Last-minute Christmas shopping.

Mother's Pride
or The Nose Picker of Bethlehem

My son, he was the shepherd in the school nativity,
A part I feel he played with style and sensitivity.
And right from the beginning, he stood out above the crowd . . .
From when he whispered, 'Someone's nicked my lamb' a trifle
  loud.

I guess he must had felt the time had come to improvise
When he pulled up his costume to reveal his chubby thighs.
Though they are quite delectable, his timing did not seem
Appropriate to the atmosphere of the moving stable scene.

His one line was delivered in a most dramatic way;
I'm sure that many shared my thought, 'A star is born today'.
But I'd have felt a touch more misty-eyed, all truth to tell,
Had he refrained from picking his nose right through 'The First
  Noël'.

The strain of live performing took its toll, as we all saw,
When he poked Mary with his crook, it caused quite a furore.
But when at last that curtain fell, my cheeks were all aglow . . .
For I felt, quite objectively, that my son stole the show.

Turkeyed-Out

We had it hot, we had it cold,
We had it fricassée,
We turned it into curry . . .
Then Malaysian Satay.
But by day six, I must confess
I needed inspiration;
I scanned my gourmet cook books
For a turkey-based sensation.
I found the rissoles, soups and quiche,
The turkey breast *en croûte*,
And little devilled 'turkey bites'
(With spicy dip to boot!)
A tangy turkey salad
And a turkey casserole
And a festive variation . . .
Toad and turkey in the hole.
And as we saw the New Year in
With turkey, it seemed clear
Why no one ever eats the stuff
Except for . . .
Once a year.

Office Party

We knew that Mandy from Accounts would try
To get off with that Wayne from Personnel,
But little did she know that 'Dishy Di'
From Sales, she had the hots for him as well.
Soon pints and rums and cokes had been consumed,
Soon Di and Wayne were urgently entwined,
While devastated Mandy sat and fumed
And hissed things like, 'My God, he must be blind'.
Then enter hunky John from Engineering
And quickly mournful Mandy caught his eye,
Soon thoughts of wanton Wayne were disappearing
As Mandy got absorbed by her new guy.
More drinks were drunk and friendships consummated
While in four homes, four spouses sat and waited.

The Joy of Giving or . . .
Presents Imperfect

Aunt Mary did not like her peach bath foam,
She said, 'It's bound to give me such a rash.'
And Helen, barely ten, was heard to groan,
'I hate books. Next year please just give me cash.'
John's jumper had to go back to the shop,
'The sizing must be wrong' we all concluded,
And baby's leaping frog was . . . well . . . a flop
For sadly batteries were not included.
I thought Jim very tactless, truth to tell
When he yelled out, 'Oh no, not socks again.'
But luckily our Betty took it well
When she received Eau de Toilette . . . for men!
I have to say my mum was very miffed,
And made her deep displeasure very clear,
When she unwrapped her favourite niece's gift
And found the vase she'd given her last year.
And Dad he didn't even bat an eye
And somehow even forced a sort of grin,
When for the third year running, lucky guy,
He got *Chess For Beginners; Play to Win.*

Yes Christmas is indeed a time for giving
But things can go awry, and it helps when
There's twelve months for forgetting and forgiving
Till present swapping time comes round again.

Festive Joys

Yes Christmas day is drawing nigh,
I've lots of presents still to buy,
I yield a most un-festive sigh,
Pre-Christmas stress. I'm going to cry.

A dozen mince pies yet to make,
The icing has slid off my cake,
I burnt the pudding by mistake,
This frazzled female needs a break.

Wrapped parcels scattered on the floor.
Forgot the labels. What a bore;
Now no idea who they are for.
Unwrap the whole lot to make sure.

A dozen jobs still not begun
And endless errands still to run,
Yes, at this time of festive fun
A woman's work is never done.

But we forge on. We won't be beat.
No way will we admit defeat.
We won't put up those weary feet
Till gifts are given and guests replete.

Those days when I felt fraught and stressed
I really never would have guessed
I'd make it. Yes I'm quite impressed!
And now . . .
Can I please have a
REST!